FAITH, FABLES, FOOEY!

FAITH, FABLES, FOOEY!

AN IRREVERENT LOOK AT ORGANIZED RELIGION

E.B. ROBAIRE

ILLUSTRATED BY CAMILLE DAVIES

Faith, Fables, Fooey!: An Irreverent Look at Organized Religion
Published by Island Soul Publishing
Seattle, Washington, U.S.A.

Library of Congress Control Number: 2021918050

ROBAIRE, E.B., Author
FAITH, FABLES, FOOEY!
E.B. ROBAIRE

ISBN: 978-1-7378544-0-1 (paperback)
ISBN: 978-1-7378544-1-8 (hardcover)

RELIGION / General
RELIGION / Faith

QUANTITY PURCHASES:
Schools, companies, professional groups, clubs, and other organizations may qualify for special terms when ordering quantities of this title. For information, email islandsoulpublishing@gmail.com.

This book is printed in the United States of America.

This book is dedicated to religious freedom for all.

Religious freedom is the principle that supports the freedom of any person, in public or private, to practice a religion or belief, as well; as the freedom to question one's religion or belief.

> *"The universe is a big place, perhaps the biggest."*
> — Kurt Vonnegut

What is the purpose of life?

Is there a God?

How do we define God?

What happens to us when we die?

From the dawn of man until the present time, people have pondered these age-old questions and mysteries of our universe.

Since the beginning of human time, there have been hundreds of thousands of different religions. Even today, there are many thousands of different religions.

Scientists estimate that over 100 billion people have lived through the course of human history, most of whom have gone to their grave believing theirs was the one and only true religion.

Among the most famous of the ancient religions was that of the Greeks, believed to have begun as early as 1500 BC. This religion, popularized in the Iliad and the Odyssey, encompassed a collection of beliefs that included twelve major gods and goddesses and over 400 minor gods.

The main gods resided on Mount Olympus, and each had different powers. Zeus was the king of gods, sending thunder and lightning from the skies; Poseidon ruled over the oceans. Aphrodite was the goddess of love, and Hades, brother of Zeus, ruled the underworld. Although these gods were immortal, they were not all-powerful and at times would oppose one another and even interact with mortals.

When the Romans conquered Greece beginning in 146 BC, they took much of the Greek religion and incorporated it into their own with similar beliefs, but they used their own names for each of the Gods, such as Zeus being Jupiter, Neptune instead of Poseidon, Venus rather than Aphrodite, etc.

Four major religions dominate the world's belief systems today, representing over 75% of the world's population.

These four religions include Buddhism, Christianity, Hinduism, and Islam. No other single religion accounts for more than 1% of the world population.

There are many other religions whose followers number in the millions.

In addition, those who claim no religion including atheists and agnostics, together comprise almost 14% of the world's population.

The major religions as a percent of the world population.

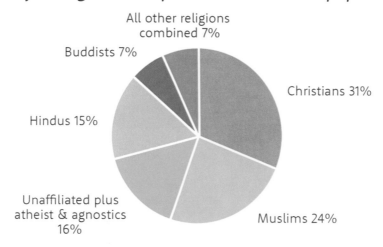

All other religions combined 7%

Buddists 7%

Christians 31%

Hindus 15%

Unaffiliated plus atheist & agnostics 16%

Muslims 24%

Number of people in 2015, in billions

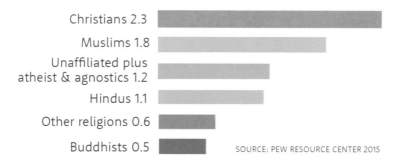

Christians 2.3

Muslims 1.8

Unaffiliated plus atheist & agnostics 1.2

Hindus 1.1

Other religions 0.6

Buddhists 0.5

SOURCE: PEW RESOURCE CENTER 2015

The number of followers of the two largest religions in the world, Christianity and Islam, together account for over half, more specifically 55%, of all of the people in the world.

The number of Hindus and Buddhists combined comprise another 22%.

Yet, many thousands of other organized religions exist today. In fact, hundreds of new religions emerge every year around the world.

"Religion is one tree with many branches. As branches, you may say religions are many, but as a tree, religions are only one."

- Mahatma Gandhi

All major religions have a number of sects or subdivisions within their religion that hold different beliefs and/or interpretations of their religious dogma.

These many subdivisions or sects often have dramatically different interpretations, beliefs, traditions, and rituals that might even lead one to assume they are completely separate religions.

There are two major sects or denominations within Islam that make up 99% of all Muslims world-wide, four major sects in Hinduism, three major denominations within Buddhism, three or four different divisions within Judaism, and though estimates vary, religious scholars estimate as many as 30,000 or more different denominations or sub religions within Christianity.

All religions claim to teach the truth. The question then is, which, if any, of these religions has the absolute truth?

Is there a God, are there multiple Gods, or is our universe the result of some accidental cosmic big bang?

If one religion does have the absolute truth, conversely, wouldn't this mean that all other religions are wrong?

Does religion really come from God (or Gods) or is organized religion merely an invention of man?

Hinduism

The oldest religion still currently practiced is Hinduism, the world's third largest religion. Estimates as to when this ancient religion was founded range from 3000 to 5000 BC.

Although Hinduism is impossible to define in a simple paragraph or two, this complex religion teaches that existence is a cycle of birth, death, and rebirth, the result of "karma," and that the soul passes through a cycle of successive lives. Each incarnation is determined by one's actions in their previous life.

Followers of most forms of Hinduism worship a single deity, known as "Brahman," but also often honor other gods and goddesses, the main ones being Vishnu, Shiva, and Brahma. Hindus believe that at least a part of "Brahman" exists in everyone and that all living creatures have a soul and are part of a supreme soul, and as such, they revere all animals.

Since one's actions and thoughts directly determine their current and future lives, the goal of a Hindu is to achieve "moksha," which one does through living a good and virtuous life. Living such a worthy life will ultimately lead to the end of the cycle of rebirth in physical form and allow one to become part of the absolute soul.

Vishnu   Shiva   Brahma

Holy Cow!

In Hinduism, killing a cow is a serious sin, and the eating of
beef is considered akin to cannibalism. As a result, stray cows
enjoy great liberties in many parts of India. They wander through
the streets, break into gardens, relieve themselves on the
sidewalks, and frequently create traffic jams. To most Hindus,
everything about them is sacred, even their dung and urine.

Even today, no pious Hindu will pass a cow without touching
it and then touching his own head as an act of homage. In some
parts of India, a person can be sent to jail for killing or injuring
a cow. Some local governments even maintain old-age homes for
animals that have become too weak to survive in the streets.

Baby Tossing

In certain regions of southern India, there is a strange annual ritual known as "baby tossing," where Hindu priests heave babies, anywhere from three months to two years old, from the rooftop of a temple onto a bedsheet held by men on the ground below. This centuries-old practice is believed to make the babies grow stronger, become more courageous, and bring future prosperity to the infants and their families.

As each screaming baby is safely caught in the blanket (at least, hopefully so), the surrounding crowd celebrates. The infant is then passed from person to person until finally returned to its mother.

Authorities and children's rights groups have been trying to get this unique tradition banned, but many devotees of this practice are resistant, feeling it's a matter of religious freedom. Thus, this terrifying ritual continues to be practiced in many villages in parts of India.

The Temple of Rats

Many people travel to Northern India to visit the famous Karni Mata temple. When they enter, they find the temple floor crawling with over twenty thousand rats that live there. These rats are believed to be reincarnations of certain dead people, eventually destined to be reborn as higher life forms. The rats move freely throughout the entire temple complex; and are provided with all the food they can eat. Visitors are required to remove their shoes and let the rodents run across their feet. The most devoted followers even drink from the bowl the rats bathe and play in. Some even sleep in the temple, letting the rats crawl over them during the night.

The majority of the rats are brown, but it is believed that four white rats also live in the temple. They are thought to be the incarnations of the four brothers of Karni Mata, and spotting one of these white rats is believed to bring good fortune.

Holy Men

It is estimated that there are as many as five million Hindu holy men in India.
These holy men are called Sadhus and also known as yogis, fakirs, or
swamis, though each of these terms has slightly different meanings.

These holy men (and some women) have given up all their possessions and
cut all family ties to devote themselves to a search for enlightenment.

They lead a life of extreme austerity and self-deprivation, spending
months, even years, in silent meditation. They eat very little food, wear
little clothing, and most abstain from sex and other earthly pleasures.

Their quest for spiritual enlightenment can take many forms. Some will
sit in a yoga posture for years at a time as they ponder the meaning of life.
Others wander naked through the forests living on fruits and berries or
exist by begging for handouts. Some use marijuana, hashish, and other
mind-altering drugs to try to reach a higher state of consciousness.

Many of these Sadhus are able to walk on hot coals,
lie on a bed of nails, or perform a myriad of other
mind-boggling feats. One particular sect, the Aghoris,
are even known to eat the flesh of the dead and then sit
on the half-eaten corpses while meditating, believing
that doing so gives them supernatural powers.

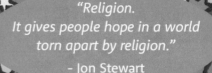

Islam

Islam is the world's second-largest religion; there are approximately 1.6 billion Muslims, accounting for almost 25% of all the people in the world. Islam originated with the teachings of Muhammad, a seventh-century Arab religious and political figure.

The word Islam means "submission," or total surrender to Allah, as Muslims refer to God. The term "Muslim" in Arabic; means "one who submits to Allah."

Muslims believe God revealed the Qur'an (the word of Allah) to Muhammad through the angel Gabriel. They consider the Qur'an and the Sunnah (words and deeds of Muhammad) as the fundamental sources of Islam.

Muhammad is considered to be the final prophet after Abraham, Moses, and Jesus (whom Muslims do not regard as God). Followers of Islam believe that the Jews and Christians distorted the revelations that God gave to these other prophets by altering the interpretation.

Muslims believe God is beyond man's comprehension. One is not expected to visualize God but to worship and adore him. The Qur'an teaches that when the world ends, Allah will judge all and decide who will go to either Jannah, "the garden of eternity," i.e. heaven, or be condemned to Jahannam, Islam's term for hell. However, in Islam, the decision of who goes to heaven or hell comes from Allah, and even those of other religions may be rewarded by Allah.

Pray All Day

Muslims around the world must perform an obligatory ritual every day known as "salah" (meaning prayer), in which they are required to recite certain prayers in Arabic five times per day while facing towards the Kaaba, the holy site in Mecca.

These prayers start at dawn and are spread throughout the day and evening so that worshippers can maintain their connection to Allah. Some stand while praying, while others kneel on prayer rugs.

It is expected for all to repeatedly bow and prostrate themselves as they recite prayers from the Qur'an, glorifying and praising Allah.

Originally, worshippers were told to pray fifty times a day, but the Prophet Musa (Moses) asked Mohammed to ask God to reduce the number, so eventually, this number was reduced to five times a day, but the reward towards being granted entrance to Jahhah, i.e. heaven, upon one's death, still counts as fifty.

Flying Donkey

In Islamic tradition, it's taught that one night Muhammad,
accompanied by the angel Gabriel, traveled up to the seven heavens
riding a white creature by the name of Burāq, which was larger
than a donkey, but smaller than a mule, with wings on its sides.

In some traditions, this creature has also been described as a
horse with the head of a woman and the tail of a peacock.

On his journey, it is told that Mohammed first prayed at the
Holy Temple before ascending to the heavens where he met
with Adam, Jesus, Joseph, Moses, Abraham, and others before
finally reaching the throne of Allah, who then gave him the
commandment and instructions for how all Muslims should pray.

Holy Trek!

One of the key traditions in Islam is the Hajj, an annual pilgrimage to Mecca, the holy city for all Muslims, considered mandatory for all adult Muslims at least once in their lifetime. This pilgrimage, associated with the life of Muhammad, includes a procession of a million or more people all converging on Mecca the same week.

During this time, each must perform a series of rituals, including tawaf, which involves circling the Kaaba (the holiest site in Islam) counter-clockwise seven times, each time kissing or touching the black stone of Mecca. This rite is believed to cleanse them of their sins.

One more important ritual is the stoning of the devil, in which one throws pebbles or rocks and must hit each of the three holy pillars (now walls) seven times. Every pilgrim must also shave their head or cut their hair. Another mandatory ritual involves the sacrifice of animals, sheep, goats, camels, etc., with the meat donated to feed the poor.

Heavenly Virgins

One controversial aspect of Islam is writings interpreted by some to mean that every devout Muslim man who dies and goes to heaven will have seventy-two houris, basically sex slaves, waiting for him in heaven for his own exclusive use.

Islamic writings describe these houris as young virgins with sparkling eyes, firm round breasts, and fair skin. They are modest and submissive in their behavior and ready to do whatever that man desires.

He may still, however, maintain a marital relationship with his earthly wife, provided she also makes it to heaven. The man, his wife, and all of his houris are believed to never again have any disagreements, and everyone will live harmoniously in a state of eternal youth, beauty, and perfect health.

Many progressive Muslims interpret this to be a metaphor, rather than a literal truth.

17

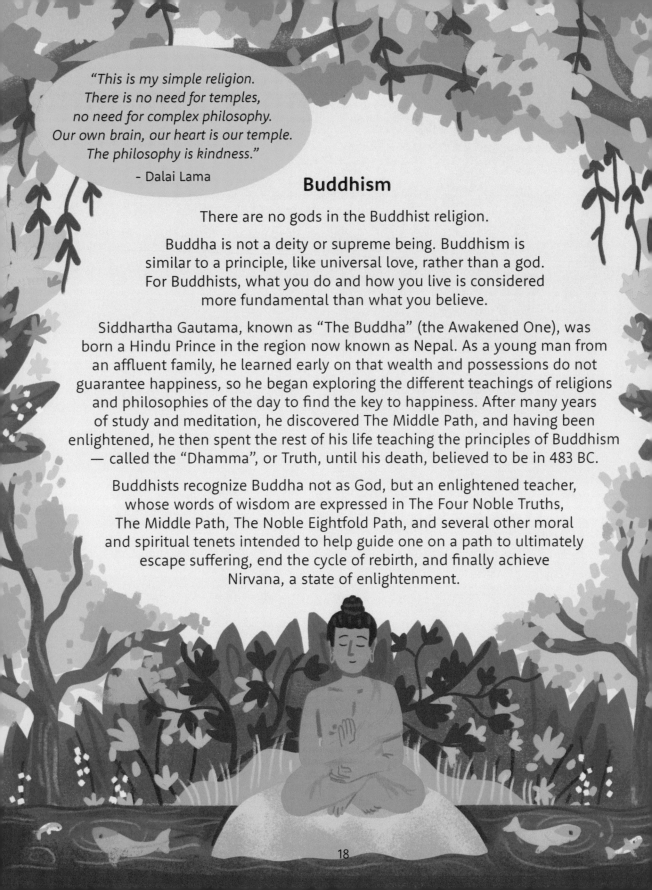

*"This is my simple religion.
There is no need for temples,
no need for complex philosophy.
Our own brain, our heart is our temple.
The philosophy is kindness."*

- Dalai Lama

Buddhism

There are no gods in the Buddhist religion.

Buddha is not a deity or supreme being. Buddhism is
similar to a principle, like universal love, rather than a god.
For Buddhists, what you do and how you live is considered
more fundamental than what you believe.

Siddhartha Gautama, known as "The Buddha" (the Awakened One), was
born a Hindu Prince in the region now known as Nepal. As a young man from
an affluent family, he learned early on that wealth and possessions do not
guarantee happiness, so he began exploring the different teachings of religions
and philosophies of the day to find the key to happiness. After many years
of study and meditation, he discovered The Middle Path, and having been
enlightened, he then spent the rest of his life teaching the principles of Buddhism
— called the "Dhamma", or Truth, until his death, believed to be in 483 BC.

Buddhists recognize Buddha not as God, but an enlightened teacher,
whose words of wisdom are expressed in The Four Noble Truths,
The Middle Path, The Noble Eightfold Path, and several other moral
and spiritual tenets intended to help guide one on a path to ultimately
escape suffering, end the cycle of rebirth, and finally achieve
Nirvana, a state of enlightenment.

Hungry Ghosts

Many Buddhists believe in Hungry Ghosts, phantom-like creatures, half-alive, half-dead, all tormented by an intense hunger. Their starving bodies are shriveled down to just skin and bone. They can't eat anything, because their mouths are the size of a pinhole and their necks extremely long and thin. As a result, they have huge, bloated bellies from starvation, which causes them to suffer severe hunger pains.

Some Buddhists believe that a man who is overly greedy in life will be punished in his next incarnation by being reborn as a Hungry Ghost. This punishment can result from various forms of greed, including gluttony, thirst for money or power, or an insatiable lust for sexual pleasures. Harmful emotions such as anger and hate can also cause a person to be reborn as a Hungry Ghost.

However, since in Buddhism nothing lasts forever, after a Hungry Ghost has endured enough suffering it will be reborn into another life form.

These Hungry Ghosts live in a kind of shadowy world and cannot normally be seen by humans. However, some say they have seen these ghosts trying to nibble on corpses, or wandering around in deserts and other wastelands.

Many Buddhists today find Hungry Ghosts to be simply a metaphor for those who follow a path of greed or who suffer from spiritual emptiness.

Burial for the Birds

A traditional custom in Tibetan Buddhism for disposal of the dead is known as the sky burial, though it's actually not a burial at all. This ritual is considered a secret and spiritual ceremony in which the bodies of the deceased are taken to a mountain top or other high elevation by a procession of monks, as they chant prayers on their journey to the "burial" site. Upon arrival, the body is then chopped up by trained "body breakers" and left for the vultures, considered to be angel-like figures that will take the souls to the heavens where they await reincarnation.

In this religion, it is believed that the soul moves on from the body at the very instant of death, so there is no longer an attachment to the physical body. In order for the soul of the person to have an easy transition into their next life, the Tibetans believe there should be no trace left of the physical body after death.

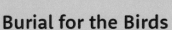

Sikhism

Sikhism is the fifth-largest religion in the world, with over 25 million followers. The word "Sikh" means "disciple" in Punjabi, as Sikhs consider themselves the disciples of God who follow the writings and teachings of the Ten Sikh Gurus.

Sikhism was founded in the late fifteenth century in the Punjab region, in what is now India and Pakistan. It is based on the spiritual teachings of Guru Nanak, the first Guru, and the nine Sikh Gurus that succeeded him. Sikhism believes in one God, without form or gender, who exists in every person's soul. They believe that all people, regardless of race or religion, are equal in the eyes of God.

Sikhism believes that the soul goes through many cycles of birth, death, and rebirth before reaching human form.

Sikhs do not believe in superstitions or rituals. They do, however, keep their hair uncut or natural, and the men have beards and wear turbans, a practice considered a mandatory sign of their faith.

21

Christianity

Christianity is the worlds' largest religion, representing approximately 30 percent of the world's population.

The majority of Christian religions believe in one God, the Father, Son, and Holy Ghost, who created heaven, earth, and the universe. These beliefs are based on the writings of the New Testament that tells the story of the Holy Spirit impregnating a Jewish virgin named Mary, who lived in Bethlehem thousands of years ago. Sometime after being impregnated, though still somehow remaining a virgin, Mary married her intended, Joseph, a Jewish carpenter. Mary then gave birth to Jesus, the son of God and the "Messiah" or savior of the world. It is believed by Christians that Jesus was sent by God so that people's sins would be forgiven and they would be given salvation and eternal life.

As Jesus grew up, his teachings and claims to be the Messiah upset the Jewish leaders of that time and threatened the Romans politically due to his strong following. Thus, with encouragement from these Jewish leaders, the Romans crucified Jesus on a cross. On the third day after his crucifixion, Mary Magdalene, a former prostitute and follower of Jesus, found the huge stone in front of the cave rolled away and the tomb of Jesus empty. The apostles, also all Jewish, then believed Jesus was resurrected, i.e. he rose from the dead and soon-after ascended up to heaven.

After Jesus' crucifixion and resurrection, it's believed that God's presence remained on earth in the form of the Holy Spirit to be a comfort to all.

The Old Testament

The Christian Bible consists of the Old Testament and the New Testament.

The Old Testament, also known as the Hebrew Bible, plays an important part in both the Christian and Jewish religions. Originally written in Hebrew, scholars believe the Old Testament was written by as many as forty different people, possibly over as many as fifteen hundred years, beginning as early as 1400 BC, with the last book completed sometime between 100 to 200 AD.

The Old Testament is a collection of sixty-six to seventy-three different books, depending on the religion.

Some interpret the Bible literally, while others believe it consists of stories, fables, and metaphors. The Old Testament states that Adam and Eve were the first human beings, created 10,000 years ago. However, scientific studies have since proven that the first humans, Homo sapiens, date back as far as 200,000 years.

HOLY BIBLE
OLD TESTAMENT

The New Testament

The New Testament is believed to have been written by a number of different people dating back as early as 40 AD and as late as 140 years after the death of Jesus. The New Testament includes a collection of twenty-seven texts, approximately half the size of the Old Testament. It contains four accounts of Jesus's life and ministry, known as the Gospels, the Acts of the Apostles, letters attributed to the Apostle Paul and other early church leaders, and a book of apocalyptic prophecy, Revelation.

Most religious scholars agree that the Gospels do not contain any eyewitness accounts.

Although Jesus and his disciples spoke Aramaic, the New Testament was originally written in Koine Greek, an ancient form of Greek language. The New Testament was translated into Latin in the fourth century AD and was not translated into English until 1526.

It's not surprising, considering that the New Testament is a collection of books, translated from ancient languages, written thousands of years ago by many different people over a period of a hundred years or more, that there are so many contradictory passages to be found in it.

This may also explain why there are so many different interpretations and thus, so many subdivisions or sects within the Christian religion.

Bible Stories

There are countless stories in the Bible describing events we don't normally encounter today, such as talking snakes, donkeys, trees, and bushes; Noah fathering three sons when he was 500 years old; Jonah living inside a whale; Samson possessing supernatural strength and slaying 1,000 enemies with the jawbone of an ass, then losing his strength after a haircut; and many more farfetched stories too extensive to list here.

However, what may be even harder to comprehend are the many stories in the Bible describing God's angry and vengeful actions such as how he ordered people to sacrifice or even eat their own children, sent bears to maul forty-two small boys for simply mocking a man, "smote" a half million firstborn sons in Egypt, purposely drowned thousands in the flood of Noah, killed thousands upon thousands of Canaanites, Israelites, Ethiopians, Syrians and more in wars, floods, plagues and other acts of genocide, murder, and mutilation.

In fact, religious scholars estimate there are well over one hundred references in the Bible in regard to God killing or ordering several million or more people killed, and yet the Bible tells us that God authored the commandment, "Thou Shall Not Kill."

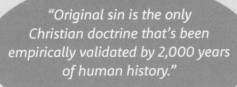

Born A Sinner

The concept of original sin is one of the basic foundations of Christianity and Catholicism. This is the belief that every human being is born a sinner because everyone ever born is descended from Adam and Eve, who committed the "original sin" by defying God's orders and eating the forbidden fruit in the Garden of Eden.

It is believed that Jesus was sent to die on the cross to save all those who believe in him from their sins. Catholics believe all newborn babies must be baptized to remove their original sin. In most Protestant religions, the age at which a person is baptized differs according to each particular denomination.

However, whether Catholic or Christian, it is believed that by sprinkling water on a newborn baby or dunking one at a particular age, or as many faiths believe, any age at all, being baptized will prevent that individual from suffering for all of eternity in a fiery, tortuous hell.

Believe or Burn!

According to Christian doctrine, those who do not accept Jesus Christ as their Lord and Savior will be condemned to spend eternity in Hell.

In most Christian denominations, no exceptions are made for nonbelievers, even those who have lived an otherwise virtuous life. This doctrine is why Christian missionaries through the centuries attempted to convert "heathens," or nonbelievers, and it also led to the crusades and other missionary actions resulting in many millions of nonbelievers, or infidels, being murdered in the name of Christ.

Both Christianity and the religion of Islam believe in a heaven and hell. However, in Islam, a faithful Muslim has a better chance of being granted entry to paradise, but a nonbeliever will not necessarily burn in hell. They believe Allah is forgiving and merciful and will judge all people according to their own religion as well as the actions of their life.

One can't help but wonder if promoting the fear tactics of spending eternity in a fiery and tortuous hell is the common reason these two religions are the largest in the world today.

The Rapture

Most Christians believe a day will come when Jesus will suddenly appear and miraculously pull all true Christians up to heaven to spend eternity with him. This day and belief is known as The Rapture.

All dead people who have lived good Christian lives will also be resurrected and pulled up. During this process, the bodies of the chosen will be transformed into an immortal state of perfect health, their minds freed from any tendency to do sinful things or even have sinful thoughts.

This transformation is regarded as a necessary step in preparing a saved person for entry into heaven.

What's That You Say?

There are 500 million adherents of various Pentecostal Christian denominations worldwide, nearly half as many as there are Roman Catholics. Pentecostal churches comprise the second most powerful denomination among all practicing Christians.

At many Pentecostal Christian church meetings and revivals, believers can be observed "speaking in tongues," technically termed, "glossolalia," best described as intense shouting, unintelligible babbling and speaking gibberish, dancing, and even fainting. Such seemingly odd behavior is considered proof that one is filled with God's Holy Spirit.

Dancing with the Devil

Less common than speaking in tongues, but still practiced at some Pentecostal related church meetings and revivals, is the handling of venomous snakes, often either rattlesnakes, cottonmouths, copper heads and occasionally even cobras. Church members, most often the pastors or preachers, handle these poisonous snakes, believed to be the incarnations of the devil or demons. They pick them up, often raising them in the air or dancing with them, even allowing them to crawl on their bodies to show their power over the demon.

However, if one happens to be bitten, this demonstrates a lack of faith or failure to have been filled with the Holy Spirit, and if the handler survives, he must then repent his sins.

There have been over sixty cases of death by snakebite in religious worship services documented in the United States over the past ten years. An article several years ago in National Geographic reported "If you go to any serpent-handling church, you'll see people with atrophied hands, and missing fingers."

30

Catholicism

Catholics comprise 50% of all Christians and about 16% of the world's population.

Catholicism dominated Christianity until 1517, when Martin Luther, a German monk, posted his Ninety-five Theses criticizing some Roman Catholic practices and teachings. Luther challenged two central and contrary doctrines by saying that the Bible is the central religious authority, not the Pope, and that humans may reach salvation only by their faith and not by their deeds.

These ideas sparked the Protestant Reformation, which led to a split in the Catholic Church. After a series of trials, the Pope excommunicated Luther in 1521.

Whether or not the Pope has a direct line to God continues to be the biggest divide between Protestants and Catholics. Other key differences include Roman Catholics having seven sacraments: baptism, confirmation, confession, the Eucharist, ordination, marriage, and last rites, while most Christians believe in only two, baptism and communion (although not all Protestant denominations practice communion on a consistent basis).

Also, Catholics believe in purgatory, while Protestants teach that all sins can only be forgiven by faith in Jesus Christ.

Catholics venerate Mary, the mother of Jesus Christ, while Protestant prayer most often centers on Jesus and do not pray to Mary, as Catholics do. One more difference is that Roman Catholic priests are not allowed to marry; while most Protestant religions do allow their ministers to marry.

Digest This!

Holy Communion, known as The Eucharist, is a Catholic ritual commemorating Jesus's Last Supper. At Sunday Mass each week, the priest offers parishioners a small portion of unleavened bread or crackers to eat and holy wine to drink.

It is believed that this sacred bread and wine are "transubstantiated," in other words, turned into the physical body and blood of Jesus Christ, so those who participate in this centuries-old ritual are consuming not a symbol, but what they believe to be the actual body and blood of Jesus.

Devil Be Gone!

Exorcism is the religious practice of evicting demons or other evil spirits from a person believed to be possessed. Millions saw the famous horror movie, "The Exorcist," or read the best-selling book years ago, but likely thought this practice was purely fictional.

However, although exorcism is an ancient practice, it is still very much a part of the Roman Catholic Church's belief system as well as several other related religions. In 2018, approximately 250 priests from 50 different countries were sent to Rome to learn how to identify demonic possession and perform exorcisms.

"Beat It, Just Beat It!"

Throughout history many religions have practiced self-flagellation, a masochistic ritual of flogging oneself with whips, chains, or other instruments of pain. Even today, there are a few sects that still practice such devotional and brutal rituals.

To commemorate the Day of Ashura, many Shi'ite Muslims, the second largest sub-division within the Islamic religion, gather in massive parades to hit themselves on the back with chains, knives and other sharp objects to mourn the death of the Prophet Muhammad's grandson, Imam Hussein.

In the northern Philippines, during the week leading up to Easter, hundreds of Filipinos tie ropes around their arms and legs, cut themselves with a blade, and then repeatedly whip their backs raw, profusely bleeding in the process. On Good Friday, hundreds of barefoot Filipinos can be seen marching through the streets in procession carrying heavy wooden crosses. All of this painful self-punishment is intended to commemorate the suffering of Jesus Christ.

Church of Jesus Christ of the Latter-day Saints

The Church of Jesus Christ of the Latter-day Saints was founded by Joseph Smith in 1830. The followers of this religion, commonly referred to as Mormons, believe Smith was a prophet who was shown golden plates by the angel Moroni in his dreams. Smith then uncovered these plates near his home in Palmyra, NY. After a revelation from God, Smith translated the sacred text on the plates, written by ancient prophets who lived from 600 BC to 400 AD, and completed their holy book, The Book of Mormon.

Documents from that time show that Smith was arrested over forty times on various charges including treason, threatening a public official, assault and battery, fraud, and polygamy. Smith was the subject of as many as forty-six lawsuits, including defrauding home-owners by claiming he had a magical "seer stone" that could discover hidden treasures. When imprisoned in 1844, while awaiting charges of inciting a riot, he and his brother were murdered by an angry mob.

Brigham Young, an apostle of Smith's, who had 55 wives then took over the leadership of the church and led the Mormons on a long exodus, eventually arriving in Utah where they waged war against the U.S. Many of Young's descendants later became LDS church leaders.

The Golden Plates

The Golden plates that Joseph Smith uncovered in the hills near his home were engraved in an ancient language. Smith, guided by the power of the Holy Ghost, used a special rock called a seer stone to translate the plates. The plates describe a race of giants, known as Nephilim, an ancient people who resulted from the interbreeding of the sons of gods and women who once roamed the earth. It is believed these giants lived in the United States many hundreds of years before the Native Americans did. The plates also describe God as having once been a mortal man from another planet who died and was resurrected.

Smith also taught, and LDS followers believe, that the original Garden of Eden was actually in Missouri, not in the Middle East.

Multiple Worlds, Gods and More...

Most of us know that Mormons are expected to refrain from indulging in alcohol, tobacco, coffee, sodas, and many other common pleasures, but that's certainly not the end of it. The fact is, there are so many odd beliefs in the LDS religion that an entire book could probably be written on just this one religion alone.

The LDS church gospel teaches that there are many other worlds that exist with people living on them and that if one spends their life doing good deeds, they can obtain the highest level and become a God themselves and have their own world or planet to rule when they die. However, everyone is still subject to only one supreme God, who resides on a planet named Kolob. This planet was God's first creation and it is the center of the universe.

The LDS religion also believes that God, Jesus, and the Holy Spirit are separate beings and that God and Jesus each have bodies of "flesh and bone", but the Holy Spirit does not, it is only a spirit.

Another unique belief is that Mormons believe in living prophets, human beings who are like Abraham, Moses, and the Apostles and who are able to receive revelation from God on both religious and practical issues. Mormons regard the President of the Church of Jesus Christ of Latter-day Saints to be one of these living prophets, with a direct link to God.

Some of these beliefs are controversial and confusing even among many LDS church members.

Holy Underwear!

In the major denomination of the Church of Latter-day Saints, faithful Mormon adults who have received the ordinance of the temple are expected to wear special "temple garments" under their clothing at all times of the day and night, to remind them of the commitment they made to God and serve as a sign of their fidelity and faithfulness.

Mormons are taught that by putting on "the armor of God," a biblical metaphor, that this sacred white underwear will protect them from fire and bullets and all temptation and evil.

> *"I distrust those people who know so well what God wants of them, because I've noticed it always seems to coincide with their own desires."*
>
> - Susan B. Anthony

Ticket to Heaven

While tithing (the giving of money) is common to many, if not most religions, it is considered mandatory in the LDS religion for members to donate 10% of their income. Otherwise, they will not be allowed into the highest kingdom of heaven. As a result of the vast majority of members tithing, the Church of the Latter-day Saints has become one of the world's wealthiest religious organizations.

Baptism of the Dead

The Church of Jesus Christ of Latter-day Saints is the only major religion that baptizes the dead. Members of this religion will often ask the church priests to baptize their deceased relatives if they have not already been baptized.

Mormon priests are also known to baptize those outside of their religion, even victims of the Holocaust, including such noted Jews as Anne Frank and Simon Wiesenthal, the famous "Nazi hunter", and thousands of others. Obviously, these baptisms were not looked upon favorably by Jewish leaders, who consider this to be highly disrespectful to their religion.

LDS baptisms have also been performed on a number of famous people and historical figures, including Humphrey Bogart, Marilyn Monroe, Elvis Presley, Joan of Arc, Gandhi, Abraham Lincoln, Pope John Paul ll, and numerous other deceased celebrities and historical figures, even though these people usually had their own religion and had absolutely no ancestral ties to the Mormon religion.

Mormons believe that baptizing these non-Mormons will allow these spirits to join the LDS religion and thus gain access to God and heaven. However, many non-Mormons strongly object to this practice and feel that the LDS church baptizes those not of their religion so that they can add to their numbers as well as claim these famous people as their own.

Amish Traditions

The Amish faith is one of the fastest-growing Christian denominations in the U.S. As with most religions, there are several sub-groups within the Amish faith, each with different customs, traditions, and practices.

While most Amish do not embrace technology; some groups do allow for the use of electricity, cars, tractors, and even cell phones. However, such usage is strictly for business purposes and not for social entertainment.

Some common Amish beliefs and traditions include not allowing their children to go to school beyond the eighth grade and not allowing their members to listen to music or play musical instruments. Church members are also not allowed to pose for photos.

Most Amish dress in plain, home-made clothing in dark colors, without buttons, zippers, etc. The men are required to grow beards, but mustaches are not allowed, and women are not allowed to cut their hair.

A famous Amish tradition is Rumspringa, a time when teenagers are encouraged to date and to question whether they want to be baptized and accept the authority of the church or leave the religion entirely.

If a church member decides to leave their community for a significant period of time, they will then be excommunicated, shunned and never allowed to return.

No Blood for you!

A fundamental doctrine of the Jehovah's Witnesses teaches that the Bible prohibits the consumption, storage, and transfusion of blood, even in the case of an emergency. This doctrine was introduced in 1945 and is accepted by a majority of Jehovah's Witnesses.

This practice has obviously drawn much criticism from the medical community as well as a small number of Jehovah's Witnesses. In 1964, this edict was even extended to include pets.

NO BLOOD TRANSFUSION

Sorry, Heaven's Full!

Another unique belief of Jehovah's Witnesses is that only 144,000 faithful Christians will be resurrected to live in heaven and rule with Jesus. These chosen ones will serve along with Jesus as kings and priests for 1,000 years and rule over the "new earth." All other faithful followers and believers will spend eternity on this new earth, which will become a paradise.

Doctor NO!

The Church of Christ, Scientist, was founded by Mary Baker Eddy in 1879 in New England. Christian Scientists do not "believe" in doctors or medical science and do not accept medical care for themselves, nor do they permit it for their children. They believe they can heal themselves through prayer, and that sin, sickness, and death do not exist; people only think they do. According to Christian Science beliefs, humans are subject to the laws of matter, only so long as they believe they are real.

Though the Church has somewhat modified their stance on the use of modern medicine over the past years, studies indicate that the cancer death rate for Christian Scientists is still almost twice that of non-believers and that no less than 6% of Christian Science deaths per year were medically preventable.

Judaism

Judaism is regarded as the world's oldest monotheistic religion, dating back nearly 4,000 years. Abraham is considered the father of Judaism because he first promoted the idea that there was only one God and that all people are created in the image of God and deserve to be treated with dignity and respect.

The Torah, the sacred book of the Jewish faith, is made up of the first five books of the Hebrew Bible, believed to be dictated to Moses by God on Mount Sinai to show the Jewish people how God wants them to live.

Today, there are about 15 million Jews worldwide, with most living in the United States and Israel. Almost 6 million Jews, close to half of all Jews in the world at that time, were murdered by the Nazis during the Holocaust.

The three main sects within Judaism are Orthodox, Conservative, and Reform, all with quite different beliefs, traditions, and rituals. Orthodox Judaism, the most extreme of these, accounts for less than 10% of the world-wide Jewish population. The Orthodox is further divided into several more sub-groups including the Hasidic. The men are recognized as having long beards and side curls and wearing wide-brimmed hats and long black coats.

Most Orthodox Jews believe that their Messiah hasn't yet come, but will one day. However, the majority of Jews do not believe in a Messiah.

Wine is Fine, but Please No Swine!

The Orthodox and ultra-Orthodox subdivisions of the Jewish religion observe strict kosher laws, known as Kashrut. These dietary laws are comprised of a list of animals that may not be eaten, including pigs, shellfish, reptiles, birds of prey, and more. They also describe how an animal should be slaughtered. These laws further mandate that no meat should be eaten with dairy, and any utensils or dishes that have even come into contact with both meat and dairy or any non-kosher food may not be used.

These kosher laws are also practiced by approximately thirty percent of the Conservative Jewish population, but are rarely observed by the majority of Reformed or Progressive Jews.

Choking the Chicken

Kaparot, a traditional Jewish religious ritual, takes place in ultra-Orthodox communities around the time of the High Holidays. It involves grasping a live chicken by the shoulder blades and swinging it over the heads of the faithful three times, symbolically transferring one's sins to the chicken.

The chicken is then slaughtered and donated to the poor, preferably eaten at the pre-Yom Kippur feast. Animal rights organizations have recently begun to picket public observances of kaparot, particularly in Israel.

47

"If all the beasts were gone, men would die from a great loneliness of spirit, for whatever happens to the beasts also happens to man. All things are connected."

- Chief Seattle of the Suquamish Tribe

Life Preservers!

Jainism, with over 4 million followers, teaches as one of its most important doctrines not to do any harm to other living beings. This instruction, known as "ahimsa", prohibits the harming of even the tiniest insects.

As a result, Jain monks will carefully sweep or clear any ants or other insects from their path before taking a step forward. Many even refuse to eat honey, since removing it from a hive might cause some of the bees to starve to death.

Such a strict observance of ahimsa obviously isn't practical for all, so most Jains observe a less-strict form in which they adhere to a vegetarian diet and oppose the killing of any animals.

Science Fiction, Cult, or Religion?

There's often a fine line between what is a religion and what is a cult. An example is Scientology, founded in the 1950s by L. Ron Hubbard, science fiction author of the best-selling book, "Dianetics." Many of Scientology's beliefs are kept secret, even to members of this Church until they have advanced into the higher tiers of this "religion" and have spent many thousands of dollars. However, these beliefs have now been exposed by many former church members.

A core belief in Scientology describes how Xenu, once ruler of the Galactic Confederacy, an ancient organization of 76 planets that existed for 20 million years, fearing he'd be thrown out of power, froze billions of souls, called "thetans" and transported them to Earth in a DC8-looking space ship, where he proceeded to dump these souls at the bottom of volcanoes and then destroyed them using nuclear bombs, killing all but a few and sending their souls into the air.

There are a number of famous celebrities who are members, including Tom Cruise, John Travolta, Kirstie Alley and dozens more. There are also abundant rumors and mysteries surrounding this so-called religion including sworn statements and lawsuits from a number of defectors regarding charges of physical abuse, brain-washing, forced labor, child abuse, rape, intimidation, and more. Former members claim they were required to disassociate with any family members who were not willing to also become Scientologists.

Religion or Cult?

Most experts agree the key difference between a religion and a cult is that a religion has lasted for generations, while a cult has not. Based on this definition, it would mean that every religion first started as a cult.

Early Christianity was considered a cult by both Jews and Romans; Islam was long viewed as a cult by medieval Christians, and even many Christ-related religions, including Baptists, Jehovah's Witnesses, Mormons, Quakers, and more were and still are considered cults by many "main-stream" Christians.

Researchers believe that as many as 5,000 cults exist today in the U.S. alone and over 20,000 around the world. The thing all these cults have in common is that their members are convinced theirs is the one and only true religion.

Drinking the Kool-Aid

A prime example of a cult is the Peoples Temple, founded by the Reverend Jim Jones in Indianapolis in the 1950s. Affiliated with the Christian Church, branches were later opened in San Francisco, L.A., and elsewhere. Ultimately, Jones, the charismatic leader of this cult, led his congregation to Guyana, where residents joined together in a mass rite of murder and suicide, resulting in the deaths of over 900 members, including men, women, and children.

Another infamous cult was the Branch Davidians, an offshoot of the Seventh-day Adventist Church, led by Vernon Howell, aka David Koresh. Koresh convinced his followers that he was anointed by God to prepare for the imminent return of Jesus. This group made headlines in 1993 when government authorities raided their compound near Waco, TX, due to suspected child abuse and other illicit activities. After a lengthy stand-off with the FBI resulting in several agents being killed, the compound was burned to the ground, and some 80 members of the group, including Koresh, were found dead.

Some believe the infamous and murderous Manson Family was a cult and of course, no list of cults would be complete without Heaven's Gate, led by university professor Marshall Applewhite. Applewhite convinced followers that the end of the earth was near, and they needed to board a spaceship and trail the Hale-Bopp Comet, but first, they must shed their earthly bodies. In 1997, 39 Heaven's Gate "believers" were found dead, after drinking a mixture of pineapple juice, vodka, and cyanide, all wearing black clothing and Nike tennis shoes.

Too Many to Believe

No book could possibly be large enough to name and describe every religion in the world. There are just far too many to list. Some of these religions, though less known than the major religions, including Taoism, Baha'i Faith, Shintoism, Confucianism, Zoroastrianism, Cao Dai, and Tenrikyo, have more than one million adherents.

There are lesser-known religions whose followers number in the thousands, such as Rastafarianism, Druidism, Asatru, Falon Gong, Soka Gakkai, and more obscure religions with hundreds of believers. Then, finally, there are a seemingly infinite number of religions with only a few dozen adherents.

Such religions include Jediism, based on the Star Wars movies, whose members believe in a Living Force that flows around and through all living beings or the increasingly popular Church of the Spaghetti Monster, also known as Pastafarianism. This so-called religion started as a parody but has since gained over one hundred thousand followers in dozens of different countries around the world.

There is the Prince Phillip Movement, a religious sect founded on the South Pacific island of Vanuatu which worships Prince Phillip, the Duke of Edinburgh, as a divine being. And let's not forget Raelism, founded by a French race-car driver in the 1970's who claimed he was abducted by aliens and taken to a distant planet called Elohim where he met Jesus, Confucius, Buddha, and other religious icons, after which he began promoting that a race of extraterrestrial scientists first created life on earth. This religion has as many as one hundred thousand members located in over ninety countries.

The seemingly endless number of religions that exist only proves that mankind is capable of believing anything. Who knows, maybe there really is a giant Flying Spaghetti Monster in the sky watching over us?

Atheism

There is a fine line in understanding the differences between atheism and agnosticism. However, neither can be considered an actual religion.

Neither atheism nor agnosticism has churches, mosques, temples, or places of worship. Neither has religious leaders. There are no hymns to be sung, no holidays to be celebrated, nor any traditions or rituals. They simply share the lack of a firm belief in a god or higher power. Atheists firmly believe there is no god or higher power, whereas agnostics believe there is no proof that a higher power exists, but they remain open to the possibility.

The word "atheism" stems from the Greek word *a* (meaning without) and *theos*, (meaning "god").

The most straightforward definition of an atheist could best be stated as one lacking in the belief of a god or god(s).

*"Regardless of your faith,
you can never escape uncertainty."*
- S. L. Alder

Agnosticism

Agnosticism can best be described by understanding the Greek word; agnostic, which means "not knowable". The term "agnostic" was first coined in 1860 by Thomas Huxley, an English biologist and an early adherent of Darwin's theory of Evolution.

Agnostics feel it is not possible to know if God(s) or any deity or higher power exists or not.

The significant difference from atheism is that an agnostic does not reject the possibility of there being a god or higher power; but feels that there is just not enough evidence or information available in order to make an informed decision. In simplistic terms, an agnostic takes the position that they cannot be sure if a god or gods exist.

Famous "Non-Believers"

The list of famous atheists and agnostics is quite extensive and includes such notable figures in history as:

Aristotle, Confucius, Lao Tzu, Andrew Carnegie, Clarence Darrow, Emily Dickinson, Benjamin Disraeli, Sigmund Freud, Ernest Hemingway, Victor Hugo, Marie Curie, Enrico Fermi, Friedrich Nietzsche, Bertrand Russell, George Bernard Shaw, Leo Tolstoy, Mark Twain, Susan B. Anthony, Oscar Wilde, Alan Turing, Nehru, Pavlov, Carl Sagan, George Bernard Shaw, Linus Pauling, Richard Leakey, W.E.B Du Bois, Robert Louis Stevenson, Franz Kafka, Emile Zola, Ayn Rand, Arthur Conan Doyle, Frank Lloyd Wright, Richard Branson, John Steinbeck, Thomas Edison, Albert Einstein, Paul McCartney, Andy Rooney, Pat Tillman, Ted Turner, Stephen Hawking, Elon Musk, Warren Buffett, Mark Zuckerberg, and many more, far too extensive to list.

Many historians feel there is evidence that many of our founding fathers and even some of our Presidents may have been atheistic or agnostic in their beliefs. This list includes: Thomas Jefferson, Benjamin Franklin, John Adams, James Madison, Ulysses S. Grant, and some scholars believe even Abraham Lincoln questioned the existence of a supreme being.

Before Recorded History

Before the invention of the printing press, which wasn't until the 15th century, there was no form of mass communication. Very few people before that time could even read or write. Communication was mostly by the spoken word, passed on by one to another.

You may have played the "telephone game" as a child. This game, in which a number of people sit around a table while one person whispers a sentence quietly in the ear of the person sitting right next to him or her. Then the next person, in turn, whispers what they thought they heard to the person next to them say and so on, until the last person has heard the sentence whispered in their ear. Finally, that very last person says aloud to all the others what they heard. The result being that what the last person finally heard is usually quite different from what the very first person whispered.

Now imagine, this same game began hundreds or even thousands of years ago and that what the first person whispered was not written down. Imagine it was whispered in a different language, then translated again to another language or to many languages over hundreds, even thousands of years' time. Imagine how different this whispered message would be after hundreds, or even thousands of years?

What are the chances that this message would remain the same as when it first started?

Most religions are based on ancient books filled with stories that were first relayed by spoken word. Yet people often take these writings literally and base their entire faith on such "information."

56

> "Beware of false knowledge,
> it is more dangerous than ignorance."
> - George Bernard Shaw

Facts or Fake News?

There is an exhaustive list of historical events, once thought to be facts, that we now know not to be true. Historical beliefs such as: George Washington had wooden teeth, Columbus discovered America, Einstein failed math in school, and Thomas Edison invented the light bulb, just to name a few.

More recently, it was believed that humans only use 10% of our brains, bats are blind, going outside in the cold with wet hair will make you sick, you'll get cramps if you go swimming right after eating, bulls get angry when they see red, and that touching a toad will give you warts. So many myths once believed to be true, but since proven incorrect, it would take a book much bigger than this in order to list them all.

Even today, many people still believe in the numerous conspiracy theories regarding the assassination of JFK, the 9/11 terrorist attack, that the Holocaust never happened, the moon landing was faked, the QAnon conspiracy is true, the 2020 election was rigged, and the list goes on. Many still even believe the earth is flat.

Given all of the "fake news" over the past years, perpetuated by politicians and the news media, who can really know what is fact and what is fake?

Even recent events, where there have been literally thousands, even millions of observers, still abound with various rumors, conspiracy theories, and opinions stated as facts, most without any factual basis whatsoever.

Many historians argue there is no actual historical evidence that Buddha, Jesus, Muhammad, or Moses even existed. This, of course, does not mean that these world-famous religious figures did not exist; it just means there is little or no documented proof of their existence.

Yet, millions of people are fully convinced that what was written in a book thousands of years ago in a different language, authored by numerous unknown people, is completely and unquestionably true.

*"Is God willing to prevent evil,
but not able? Then he is not omnipotent.
Is he able, but not willing? Then he is malevolent.
Is he both able and willing? Then whence comes evil?
Is he neither able or willing?
Then why call him God?*

- Epicurus

Why Do Bad Things Happen to Good People?

And conversely, why do good things happen to bad people?
Why do millions of babies and small children die
before they've even had a chance to live?

Why are some people born into loving families while others don't have
parents to care for them? Why do some have parents who abandon
them or, worse yet, abuse them? Why are so many born with deformities
or handicaps, while others are blessed with good looks and talent?

Why do some evil people seem to prosper, while
many good people are made to suffer?

Are these the result of God's will as many religions believe, God
working in mysterious ways as some preach, pay-back through karma
from previous lives, or is it simply a result of happenstance, chaos
or coincidence, a twist of fate, with no basis or reason at all?

What Would You Believe If...?

If you were raised in a certain religion and taught that yours
was the one true religion, it is likely this is what you believe.
Statistics indicate that approximately two-thirds of
Americans maintain the same religion as their parents.

After all, very few people come to believe in their religion on their own.
Most often, how one is raised determines one's religious beliefs.

However, ask yourself this theoretical question
and try to answer as honestly as you can:

Imagine you were born into a different religion.
Let's say you were raised in India as a Hindu
or born into a Buddhist family in Thailand
or brought up in a Muslim family in Saudi Arabia.

Now further imagine that everything that you were ever
taught about religion, from the day you were born up until
the present time, was that your family's religion was the
one and only true religion and that everyone of your friends
and everyone you knew was of this same religion.

Can you say with certainty that you would still believe what you do today?

59

The Golden Rule

The Golden Rule is the ethical principle of treating other people just as we ourselves want to be treated. All of the major religions have their own version of the Golden Rule; Though the words may differ, the meaning is absolutely the same.

The Hebrew Old Testament:
"Thou shalt love thy neighbor as thyself."

The Christian New Testament:
"Do unto others as you would have them do unto you."

Islam, the Qu' ran:
"None of you truly believes until he wishes for his brother what he wishes for himself."

Hinduism:
"Do nothing unto others which would cause you pain if done to you."

Buddhism:
"Hurt not others in ways that you yourself would find hurtful"

One cannot help but wonder what our world be like if everyone believed and practiced nothing more than these simple "golden rules?"

Author's Notes

I feel extremely fortunate to have found such a talented
artist as Camille Davies to illustrate this book. Writing and
publishing this book has taken over a year, and she was an
absolute pleasure to work with from beginning to end.

It's important that anyone who has been offended by some of the
content in this book understands that Camille had no say or involvement
whatsoever in the subject, the text, or anything other than the
illustrations. In fact, frankly, she was hesitant regarding some of the
text and had to be reminded that she was contractually bound to restrict
herself to creating the illustrations and to leave the writing to me.
Camille is a wonderful soul who would never want to offend anyone.
I take full responsibility for every word written in this book.

I've studied comparative world religions for over fifty years, and it's been
my intention for quite some time to someday write a book on the subject.
I'm not sure why, but for as long as I can remember, I've had a fascination
with trying to understand why it is that people believe as they do.

I also happen to be a firm believer in the importance
of religious freedom; that everyone has the right
to believe however they so choose, as long as it doesn't
interfere with another's right to believe differently.

I certainly cannot say, with any conviction, that any one
religion is right or wrong, nor can anyone else, being
that all religions are based on faith and not fact.

However, I do believe it is healthy to question one's beliefs.
If our beliefs cannot pass scrutiny or be subject to our asking questions,
is that religion truly worthy of our belief and faith? If there is indeed
a god, then didn't God endow us with a brain to think and reason with?

The intent of this book is not to criticize anyone's religion, but rather to ask questions of all organized religions. I realize some may be offended by the content, and I wouldn't dream of attempting to deny that this book takes a critical view of organized religion. Thus, I included a warning label on the back cover.

However, the reason religion is commonly referred to as faith is that faith, at least according to the Webster Dictionary is a firm belief in something for which there is no proof.

No one can argue that having hope and faith can be reassuring. However, hope and faith are exactly as their meanings imply. They are wishes and dreams and maybe even beliefs, but this does not make them facts.

I've never been able to understand why it's so difficult for so many to admit there is much they don't understand. I myself am clueless when it comes to understanding subjects such as nuclear physics, advanced calculus and many other complex concepts, too numerous to mention. In fact, I confess to having to struggle in just helping my seven-year-old grandson assemble his latest Lego project. How could I possibly begin to understand how our universe was created?

This is why I have such regard for those Native American tribes that referred to the creator as the "Great Spirit" or the "Great Mystery." In doing so, they were acknowledging that, as mere mortals, they were incapable of understanding all the mysteries of the universe.

Nevertheless, although these questions are impossible to answer, I admit to having a degree of faith myself. Maybe having faith is a natural human condition.

It's never made sense to me that our universe was created from chaos or that it was the result of some sort of cosmic accident. However, this is about as far a leap of faith as I'm prepared to venture. I would never think of describing my beliefs as fact.

As for believing in any ancient holy book or complex religious dogma handed down from thousands of years ago, sorry, but accepting that as the absolute truth is way too much of a reach for me. The point is, having faith is perfectly fine, but believing that your faith is the one and only true religion? Such iron-clad beliefs can only lead to dissension and conflict, as history has proven time and time again.

It is important to understand and accept that faith is not fact. If each of us understands and accepts that our religion is based on our faith and not on facts, then we also establish the basic right for others to believe as they do and hopefully, in doing so, we, in turn, do not attempt to force our faith on others. Religion is based on faith, not fact! That's precisely what this book is all about.

In closing, thank you so much for purchasing this book. I hope you enjoyed reading it and that possibly it provoked a bit of thought. If you didn't find this book to be your particular "cup of tea," no problem. At the very least you gave it a try.

I understand we don't all think alike. If we did, how boring would our world be? Let's just agree that we all have the right to believe as we so choose and, regardless of our religious leanings, live our lives just as the Golden Rule suggests, treating one another just like we ourselves want to be treated.

What a wonderful world this would be if everyone did nothing more than just this.

About the Author

E.B. Robaire graduated from university with honors in history. Having always had a strong interest in religion and wanting to understand why people believe as they do; he went on to earn his Doctorate in Divinity. He currently lives with his wife on an island in the Pacific Northwest, while continuing his studies of history and the various world religions.

When it comes to his own beliefs, Robaire quotes the famous architect, Frank Lloyd Wright, "I believe in God, only I call it Nature," acknowledging there are mysteries in our universe that mankind is incapable of understanding.

CPSIA information can be obtained
at www.ICGtesting.com
Printed in the USA
BVRC101410191221
624204BV00023B/425